The First Christmas

Luke 2:1–20

(The Birth of Jesus)

Mary Manz Simon
Illustrated by Dennis Jones

ST. LOUIS

For Beth Innes, Marti Beuschlein, Leah
Serck, and all early childhood educators
who share the Good News of Jesus Christ,
our Savior born in Bethlehem

Books by Mary Manz Simon

Hear Me Read Level 1
What Next? CPH
Drip Drop, CPH
Jibber Jabber, CPH
Hide the Baby, CPH
Toot! Toot! CPH
Bing! CPH
Whoops! CPH
Send a Baby, CPH
A Silent Night, CPH
Follow That Star, CPH
Row the Boat, CPH
Rumble, Rumble, CPH
Who Will Help? CPH
Sit Down, CPH
Come to Jesus, CPH
Too Tall, Too Small, CPH
Hurry, Hurry! CPH
Where Is Jesus? CPH

Hear Me Read Level 2
The No-Go King, CPH
Hurray for the Lord's Army! CPH
The Hide-and-Seek Prince, CPH
Daniel and the Tattletales, CPH
The First Christmas, CPH
Through the Roof, CPH
A Walk on the Waves, CPH
Thank You, Jesus, CPH

God's Children Pray, CPH
My First Diary, CPH
52 Ways to Raise Happy, Loving Kids
   Thomas Nelson Publishing

Little Visits on the Go, CPH
Little Visits 1-2-3, CPH
Little Visits with Jesus, CPH
More Little Visits with Jesus, CPH

Copyright © 1993 Concordia Publishing House
3558 S. Jefferson Avenue, St. Louis, MO 63118-3968
Manufactured in the United States of America

Library of Congress Cataloging-in-Publication Data

Simon, Mary Manz, 1948–
    The first Christmas : Luke 2:1–20 : the birth of Jesus / Mary Manz
    Simon : Illustrated by Dennis Jones
        p. cm. — (Hear me read. Level 2)
    Summary: Retells the story of Mary and Joseph's journey to Bethlehem
and the birth of Jesus in a manger there.
    ISBN 0-570-04741-2
    1. Jesus Christ—Nativity—Juvenile literature. [1. Jesus Christ—Nativity.
2. Bible Stories—N.T.]—I. Title. II. Title: Birth of Jesus. III. Series:
Simon, Mary Manz, 1948–   Hear me read. Level 2.
BT315.2.S554   1993
232.92′1—dc20   92-21372

    3   4   5   6   7   8   9   10   02   01   00   99   98   97   96   95

"'Mary, will you be all right?"
Joseph asked.
"It will be a long trip."

"I will be fine," said Mary.
"We must go to Bethlehem."

The king had ordered everyone
to register.
People had to travel to their family's
hometown to be counted.

The roads were crowded.
Some people walked.
Some rode donkeys.
Some rode in carts.

"Let's rest here," said Joseph.

Joseph helped Mary.
She would have a baby soon.
She needed to rest.

Everyone was going to register.

"Come," said Mary.
"We must go to Bethlehem."

Joseph laughed.
"We will go," he said.
"We will go soon."

Joseph and Mary traveled on the crowded roads.

Finally, Joseph said, "Here. Here is the little town of Bethlehem. We must find a place to stay."

Joseph went to an inn.
He knocked on the door.
Knock. Knock.

"No room," growled the innkeeper.

Joseph went to another inn.
He knocked on the door.
Knock. Knock.

"No room here," said the innkeeper.
Mary was getting very tired.
She needed to rest.

"We must find a place to stay,"
Mary said.

Joseph went to another inn.
He knocked on the door.
Knock. Knock.

"There is no room," said the innkeeper.
"But Mary's going to have a baby soon,"
said Joseph.
"We must have a place to stay."

"I have a stable for animals," said the innkeeper.
"It is warm.
You can stay there."

Soon Mary had her baby.
She wrapped Him in cloths.
She laid the baby in a manger.

"What child is this?" asked the innkeeper.

"Mary had her baby," Joseph said.
"Mary had a baby boy.
His name is Jesus."

Outside of Bethlehem, shepherds
watched their sheep in the fields.
Suddenly, an angel appeared.

"Do not be afraid," said the angel.
"I bring you good news.
Jesus is born.
Jesus, the Savior, is born."

"Jesus is born in Bethlehem," said
the angel.

"You will find the baby wrapped in
cloths," the angel said.

"He will be lying in a manger."

Suddenly, many angels appeared.
"Glory to God," the angels sang.
"Glory to God in the highest."

The shepherds said, "We must see
this baby.
We must go to Bethlehem."

The shepherds hurried to the little town.

"Where is He?" they asked. "Where is baby Jesus?"

"Where is He?" they asked again.
"Where is baby Jesus?"

"Here is Jesus," said Mary.
"Come see the little Lord Jesus, asleep
on the hay."

The shepherds looked.
Jesus was in the manger.
He was wrapped in cloths.
It was just as the angel had said.

"Come, let us worship Him," said
a shepherd.
"He is Christ the Lord."
The shepherds knelt down
before Jesus.

"The angel told us Jesus was born in
Bethlehem," the shepherds said.
"The angel said we would find the baby
wrapped in cloths.
The angel said the baby would be lying
in a manger."

"Yes," said Joseph.
"This is Jesus.
Christ the Savior is born."

The shepherds told everybody their good news.
They had seen the baby Jesus.

It was night, but the shepherds were not tired.

It was night, but the shepherds were not quiet.

They sang praises to God.

"Joy to the world," the shepherds sang, "the Lord is come."

Jesus is born!

About the Author
Mary Manz Simon holds a doctoral degree in education with a specialty in early childhood education. She has taught at levels from preschool through postgraduate. Dr. Simon has also authored *God's Children Pray*, the best-selling *Little Visits with Jesus, More Little Visits with Jesus, Little Visits 1-2-3, Little Visits on the Go, My First Diary,* and the Hear Me Read Level 1 Bible stories series. She and her husband, the Reverend Henry A. Simon, are the parents of three children.